INDIAN PRAIRIE PUBLIC LIBRARY
401 Plainfield Road
Darien, IL 60561

FEB 1 1 2020

# Should the
# VOTING AGE
# Be Lowered?

By Leslie Beckett

Published in 2020 by
**KidHaven Publishing, an Imprint of Greenhaven Publishing, LLC**
353 3rd Avenue
Suite 255
New York, NY 10010

Copyright © 2020 KidHaven Publishing, an Imprint of Greenhaven Publishing, LLC.

All rights reserved. No part of this book may be reproduced in any form without permission in writing from the publisher, except by a reviewer.

Designer: Deanna Paternostro
Editor: Katie Kawa

Photo credits: Cover Lisa F. Young/Shutterstock.com; p. 5 (top) Antonio Guillem/Shutterstock.com; p. 5 (bottom) Hayk_Shalunts/Shutterstock.com; p. 7 Bettmann/Contributor/Bettmann/Getty Images; p. 9 Michael Nigro/Pacific Press/LightRocket via Getty Images; p. 11 Rob Crandall/Shutterstock.com; p. 13 (top) VGstockstudio/Shutterstock.com; p. 13 (bottom) SpeedKingz/Shutterstock.com; p. 15 Prasit Rodphan/Shutterstock.com; pp. 17, 21 (inset, middle) Joseph Sohm/Shutterstock.com; p. 19 (top left, top right) Evan El-Amin/Shutterstock.com; p. 19 (bottom) adamkaz/E+/Getty Images; p. 21 (notepad) ESB Professional/Shutterstock.com; p. 21 (markers) Kucher Serhii/Shutterstock.com; p. 21 (photo frame) FARBAI/iStock/Thinkstock; p. 21 (inset, left) LightField Studios/Shutterstock.com; p. 21 (inset, right) vesperstock/Shutterstock.com.

**Library of Congress Cataloging-in-Publication Data**

Names: Beckett, Leslie, author.
Title: Should the voting age be lowered? / Leslie Beckett.
Description: New York : KidHaven Publishing, 2020. | Series: Points of view |
    Includes index.
Identifiers: LCCN 2018052211 (print) | LCCN 2018055976 (ebook) | ISBN
    9781534567276 (eBook) | ISBN 9781534529946 (pbk. book) | ISBN
    9781534567221 (library bound book) | ISBN 9781534531192 (6 pack)
Subjects: LCSH: Voting–United States–Juvenile literature. | Voting
    age–United States–Juvenile literature.
Classification: LCC JK1978 (ebook) | LCC JK1978 .B438 2020 (print) | DDC
    324.6/208350973–dc23
LC record available at https://lccn.loc.gov/2018052211

Printed in the United States of America

CPSIA compliance information: Batch #BS19KL: For further information contact Greenhaven Publishing LLC, New York, New York at 1-844-317-7404.

Please visit our website, www.greenhavenpublishing.com. For a free color catalog of all our high-quality books, call toll free 1-844-317-7404 or fax 1-844-317-7405.

# CONTENTS

# Too Young
# TO VOTE

Many young people want to do what they can to make the world a better place. They **volunteer** in their communities, write letters to government leaders about issues they care about, and use their voices to call for change. However, until they turn 18, they can't do one of the most important things a citizen can do—vote.

Some people believe there are many good reasons for the voting age in the United States to stay at 18. However, others believe it should be lowered to give younger Americans a say in how their country is run.

## Know the Facts!

When people in the United States talk about lowering the voting age, they're most often talking about lowering it to 16 years old.

Many adults believe young people don't care enough about issues in the world around them to be allowed to vote. However, young people have become leaders in movements for stronger gun control laws and equal rights for all Americans. This had led some adults to change their point of view on lowering the voting age.

# VOTING AGE

Although some people believe the voting age in the United States is too high right now, it used to be even higher! In 1971, an amendment, or change, was made to the U.S. **Constitution**. The 26th Amendment lowered the voting age in the United States from 21 to 18.

The voting age was lowered in 1971 because the United States was at war. During the Vietnam War, people as young as 18 were chosen to serve in the military. People argued that if these young adults were old enough to die for their country, they were also old enough to vote.

### Know the Facts!

In 2013, Takoma Park, Maryland, became the first city to let 16-year-olds vote in local elections. Some other U.S. cities have also lowered their voting ages for local elections.

**Protests** against the Vietnam War were often led by young students. This helped prove they were ready to vote.

POLITICIANS LIE --GI's DIE!
*youth against WAR and Fascism*

# Informed and Active
# CITIZENS

Young people have become powerful voices for change. They're using **social media platforms** to speak out about issues that matter to them, and they're joining together to call attention to problems they see in their country. Young **activists** have shown that teenagers are often just as informed, or educated, and care just as much about important issues as adult voters.

Many laws, including laws about health care, education, and gun **violence**, directly **affect** young people. Because of this, supporters of a lower voting age believe young people should have the right to vote for the people who make those laws.

### Know the Facts!

Countries around the world that allow 16-year-olds to vote include Scotland, Austria, Brazil, and Argentina.

After a deadly shooting at their school in Parkland, Florida, teenage students planned the March for Our Lives. It was held in Washington, D.C., in 2018 to call attention to the problem of gun violence in the United States. The march proved to many people that high school students are informed and active citizens who should be able to vote.

# A Matter of
# MATURITY

Young people have shown the ability to care deeply about important issues that affect voters. However, caring about issues isn't the same thing as making **mature** decisions about them. Some people argue against lowering the voting age because they think adult brains can handle making decisions better than teenage brains.

Doctors have stated that some parts of the brain aren't fully **developed** by the time a person is 16 years old. People who oppose lowering the voting age worry that 16-year-olds won't make smart decisions in the voting booth because their brains aren't ready for that kind of task.

## Know the Facts!

An American must be at least 17 years old to serve in the military and at least 18 years old to serve on a jury, which is a group of citizens who hear the facts about a legal case and make a decision in a court of law.

Voting is one of the most important things a citizen can do. Some people believe 16-year-olds wouldn't take voting **seriously**, which is why they're against lowering the voting age.

# Not That
# DIFFERENT

It's true that some parts of a person's brain don't fully develop until they reach their 20s. However, studies have found that the parts of the brain needed to make informed decisions—such as who to vote for—work just as well in 16-year-olds as they do in adults.

Teenagers and adults have other things in common, too. For example, a person who's 16 years old can work, and if they have a job, they must also pay taxes. Many people believe if a person pays taxes, they should be allowed to vote.

## Know the Facts!

In some cases, people under the age of 18 who **commit** a crime are charged as adults. Supporters of a lower voting age believe if a young person is old enough to be treated as an adult in court, they're also old enough to vote.

In the
United States,
16-year-olds can
drive, get a job,
and pay taxes,
but they still
can't vote in
most elections.

# Knowing the
# FACTS

If a person wants to make an informed decision, they need facts. Some people think teenagers don't know enough facts about how the U.S. government works to make informed decisions in the voting booth. A lower voting age would mean a greater number of voters who haven't finished high school yet, and high school is when many students take classes in U.S. history and government.

Opponents of lowering the voting age also think most teenagers don't know enough important facts about their local, state, and national leaders. They believe better civics education is needed before 16-year-olds should be allowed to vote.

### Know the Facts!

As of 2019, nine states and Washington, D.C., make students take at least one year of classes in government or civics.

Some people believe that 16-year-olds will vote for the same people their parents vote for because they don't know enough to make a different choice.

# Voter Turnout
# TROUBLE

The number of people who vote—also known as voter turnout—is a major issue in the United States. In the 2016 U.S. presidential election, only 55.7 percent of the Americans who could vote actually voted. This number is often even lower when voters aren't choosing a president.

Many people believe allowing younger people to vote could help raise voter turnout numbers. They believe the earlier people start voting, the more likely they are to keep voting every year. Also, parents and guardians may be more likely to vote, too, because they want to set a good example for their children.

## Know the Facts!

Since the voting age was lowered to 16 in Takoma Park, voter turnout for 16-year-olds and 17-year-olds has been more than twice as high as voter turnout for older age groups.

Many people see low voter turnout as a big problem in the United States. They're looking for new ways to fix this problem, including lowering the voting age.

# An Unfair
# ADVANTAGE

Most people agree that lowering the voting age would raise voter turnout numbers. However, some people think it would raise them in unfair ways.

In the United States, there are two main political parties— groups of people who hold the same general beliefs about how the government should work. Most voters belong to either the Democratic Party or the Republican Party. Younger voters are more likely to be Democrats than Republicans. This has caused some people to argue that lowering the voting age is unfair because it would help one political party more than another.

## Know the Facts!

The results of a major study of young people between the ages of 15 and 24 were shared in 2018. This study showed that 57 percent of young people had a positive view of the Democratic Party, while 31 percent had a positive view of the Republican Party.

Donald Trump

Hillary Clinton

Some young people take part in student voting during presidential election years. In 2016, students chose Democrat Hillary Clinton over Republican Donald Trump, who was elected president by adult voters that year.

# An Important
# DEBATE

As young people continue to raise their voices about important issues, the **debate** about lowering the voting age will continue, too. After learning about both sides of this debate, do you think the voting age should be lowered?

Although people have different points of view on this issue, they all generally agree that it's important for young people to be ready to vote in an informed way when they reach the voting age. You can get ready by learning as much as you can now about the government and its leaders. It's never too early to start!

## Know the Facts!

In the United States, people can't vote unless they register, or sign up, when they reach the voting age.

# Should the voting age be lowered?

## YES

- Many young people are just as informed and care just as deeply about important issues as adult voters.

- The part of the brain that controls informed decisions, such as who to vote for, is fully developed by the time a person is 16.

- Many young people pay taxes and are affected by other issues, such as gun violence, in the same way adult voters are.

- Lowering the voting age would raise voter turnout numbers for young people and their parents.

## NO

- The brains of young people aren't mature enough to make important voting decisions.

- Young people don't know enough about the government to make informed voting decisions.

- Civics education needs to be better before young people are allowed to vote.

- Lowering the voting age gives an unfair advantage to the Democratic Party because young people are more likely to agree with its views.

You can use this chart to help you develop your own informed opinion on lowering the voting age. Can you think of any other arguments or facts to add to the chart?

# GLOSSARY

**activist:** Someone who acts strongly in support of or against an issue.

**affect:** To produce an effect on something.

**commit:** To do something—often something that is wrong.

**constitution:** The basic laws by which a country, state, or group is governed.

**debate:** An argument or discussion about an issue, generally between two sides.

**develop:** To create over time. Also, to cause to grow bigger or more advanced.

**mature:** Having the qualities of an adult.

**protest:** An event in which people gather to show they do not like something.

**seriously:** Done with care.

**social media platforms:** Websites and applications, or apps, that allow users to interact with each other and create online communities.

**violence:** The use of force to harm someone.

**volunteer:** To do something to help because you want to do it.

# For More
# INFORMATION

## WEBSITES

### Kids Voting USA: Family Fun

*kidsvotingusa.org/index.php/family-fun*
This part of the Kids Voting USA website has a list of games and activities for kids and their families to do to learn more about voting and the U.S. government.

### Vote16USA

*vote16usa.org*
Vote16USA is a movement to lower the U.S. voting age to 16 years old, and its website features arguments for a lower voting age and ways you can get involved if you feel strongly about this issue.

## BOOKS

Hunt, Samantha. *Why Do We Vote?* New York, NY: Gareth Stevens Publishing, 2018.

Nelson, Kristen Rajczak. *What Is Voting?* New York, NY: PowerKids Press, 2019.

Spilsbury, Louise. *Vote for Me!: How Governments and Elections Work Around the World*. Hauppauge, NY: B.E.S. Publishing, 2018.

**Publisher's note to educators and parents:** Our editors have carefully reviewed these websites to ensure that they are suitable for students. Many websites change frequently, however, and we cannot guarantee that a site's future contents will continue to meet our high standards of quality and educational value. Be advised that students should be closely supervised whenever they access the Internet.

# INDEX